Why Do Snakes Hiss?

And Other Questions about Snakes, Lizards, and Turtles

by JOAN HOLUB

illustrations by Anna DiVito

PUFFIN BOOKS

PUFFIN BOOKS
Published by Penguin Group
Penguin Young Readers Group,
345 Hudson Street, New York, New York 10014, U.S.A.
Penguin Books Canada Ltd, 10 Alcorn Avenue, Toronto, Ontario, Canada M4V 3B2

First published in the United States of America by Dial Books for Young Readers and Puffin Books,
divisions of Penguin Young Readers Group, 2004

1 3 5 7 9 10 8 6 4 2

LIBRARY OF CONGRESS CATALOGING-IN-PUBLICATION DATA

Holub, Joan.
Why do snakes hiss? : and other questions about snakes, lizards,
and turtles / by Joan Holub ; illustrations by Anna DiVito.
p. cm.
ISBN 0-8037-3000-4 (hardcover)—ISBN 0-14-240105-6 (pbk.) 1. Reptiles—Miscellanea—Juvenile
literature. 2. Snakes—Miscellanea—Juvenile literature. [1. Reptiles—Miscellanea. 2. Snakes—
Miscellanea. 3. Questions and answers.] I. DiVito, Anna, ill. II. Title.
QL644.2.H658 2004 597.9—dc22 2003064948

Puffin® and Easy-to-Read® are registered trademarks of Penguin Group (USA) Inc.

Manufactured in China
Set in ITC Century Book

Reading Level 3.3

Photo Credits

Front Cover, pages 1, 4, 6, 8, 11-12, 18-19, 22 (chameleon and anole), 27, 32, 34, 35, 39, 41; copyright ©
Dorling Kindersley; pages 5, 14, 15, 29, 40, 47 (hawks-bill sea turtle); copyright © Digital Vision; page 7
copyright © K.H. Switak/Photo Researchers Inc.; page 9 copyright © Creatas; page 16 copyright © F.
Stewart Westmorland/Photo Researchers Inc.; page 20, 42, 43, 44 copyright © Corel; page 21, 27, 31 copyright © Digital Stock; page 22 (iguana) copyright © Ryan McVay/Picture Quest; page 23 copyright ©
Silver Burdett Gin; page 24 copyright © Gary Vestal/Natural Selection Photography; page 25 copyright ©
Micael Nichols/National Geographic Image Collection; page 30 copyright © Zig Leszczynski; page 36 (bog
turtle) copyright © Jason Tesauro/New Jersey Division of Fish, Game, and Wildlife; page 36 (leatherback
turtle) copyright © Robert Caputo/Aurora & Quanta Productions Inc.; pages 37, 48; copyright © Arthur
Tilley/Getty Images; page 47 (horned lizard) copyright © Rod Planck/Photo Researchers Inc.

Note: The information in this book is not complete and is not intended to provide professional advice
regarding appropriate care, food, housing, toys, or games for your pet, or advice concerning the suitabili-
ty of any of these pets for your family. Consult an expert at your pet store and your vet for more complete
information about the pets in this book before purchasing these pets or any supplies for them. These pets
may bite, scratch, inject poison, carry disease or bacteria such as salmonella, or provoke allergic reactions.
Consult your doctor in the event of injury or allergic reaction. It is inadvisable to try to tame poisonous reptiles or for many wild reptiles to become pets.

Some reptiles are considered dangerous or are endangered species. Review state, city, and local laws in
your area before purchasing one of these pets, since it may be illegal or require special permits in some
locations to own some of the reptiles mentioned in this book.

For Brent Williams—J.H.
For Andrew J. Mulligan—A.D.

Box Turtle

Many people like snakes, lizards,

and turtles.

They are the most popular pet reptiles.

But some people are afraid of them!

Other well-known reptiles are

crocodiles, alligators, and tortoises.

All reptiles have scaly skin

and are cold-blooded.

4

Chameleon

How are reptiles born?

Almost all reptiles hatch from eggs.

A baby snake, lizard, or turtle

has a sharp tooth called an egg tooth.

It uses this to crack open its eggshell.

Newborn reptiles are called hatchlings.

They can take care of themselves

as soon as they hatch.

Turtle Hatchling

Snake Hatchling

Iguana Hatchling

Snakes

Red-Tailed Racer

How many kinds of snakes are there?

There are about 2,600 kinds of snakes. Some well-known snakes are king snakes, garter snakes, cobras, pythons, and rattlesnakes.

Python

What are the biggest and smallest snakes?

The longest snake

is the reticulated python

(reh-TIK-yu-lay-ted PI-thon).

It can grow up to

thirty-three feet long.

An anaconda is the thickest snake.

The biggest one ever found

measured forty-four inches around.

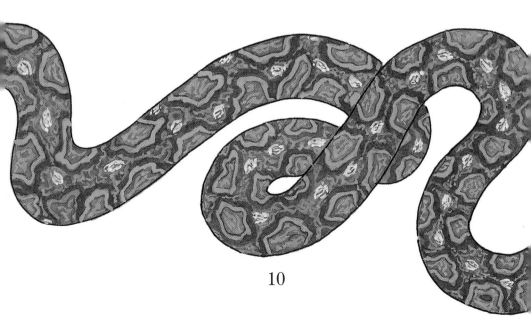

Anaconda

A thread snake is the smallest snake.

It is only about four inches long and

is as thin as a toothpick.

Snakes never stop growing.

The longer a snake lives, the bigger it gets.

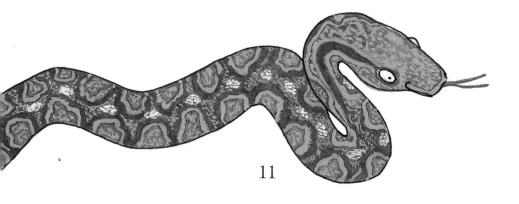

Milk Snake

Why do snakes shed their skin?

Snakes shed their skin
when they outgrow it.
This is called molting.
The old skin breaks open
and turns inside out
in one piece as the snake
moves forward and out of it.
Snakes molt several times a year.

Why do snakes hiss?

Some snakes hiss or make other noises

to scare enemies away.

A rattlesnake shakes the end

of its tail to make a rattling sound

that warns: Leave me alone!

A corn snake moves its tail

in dry leaves to make a rattling sound.

This can trick an enemy into thinking

it's a poisonous rattlesnake!

Do all snakes have fangs?

Most snakes have four rows
of small, pointed teeth
in the top of their mouths
and two rows in the bottom.
Only poisonous snakes have
sharp, hollow teeth called fangs.
The fangs of some snakes fold in
along the tops of their mouths.
When the fangs are needed,
they flip down and inject poison.

Rattlesnake

Spitting Cobra

Are all snakes poisonous?

Most snakes are not poisonous

but may bite to protect themselves.

Sea snakes are the most poisonous snakes.

Other poisonous snakes include

rattlesnakes, adders, copperheads,

cottonmouths, and cobras.

Spitting cobras can spit poison

as far as seven feet away!

Green Tree Python

How do snakes eat?

A snake can open its jaws wide enough
to eat something three times bigger
than its own head.
Snakes swallow their prey whole.

Muscles push the food along

inside the snake,

where it sits like a lump until it's digested.

It can take weeks for a snake

to digest a large meal.

A boa constrictor (BO-uh con-STRIKT-ur)

squeezes its prey

until it dies from lack of air.

Then it eats it.

How do snakes move?

Snakes push their bodies

against rough ground to move.

They can't travel across smooth surfaces,

such as ice or glass.

Most snakes can't go backward.

They have to turn around

to move in a new direction.

Different snakes move in different ways.

Sidewinder

Some snakes throw their bodies sideways.

Some grip the ground

with their muscles and scales

to creep along in a line.

Other snakes coil up,

then stick out their heads

to pull the rest of their bodies forward.

Some snakes move like a wave.

Almost all snakes can swim.

How well can snakes smell, see, and hear?

Smell is a snake's most important sense.

A snake smells mostly with its tongue,

not its nose.

Its tongue darts out

to take smells into its mouth.

Most snakes don't see or hear well,

but can feel the movement

and warmth of a nearby animal.

Snakes don't have eyelids that shut,

so it's hard to tell if they're asleep.

Lizards

Chameleon

Anole

Iguana

How many kinds of lizards are there?

There are about 3,000

kinds of lizards.

Some well-known lizards are geckos,

chameleons, anoles, and iguanas.

What are the smallest and biggest lizards?

The Jaragua (hah-RAH-gwah) gecko

is only three quarters of an inch long.

The Komodo dragon can grow

up to ten feet long

and weigh three hundred pounds.

That's as heavy as

six second-grade children.

Komodo Dragon

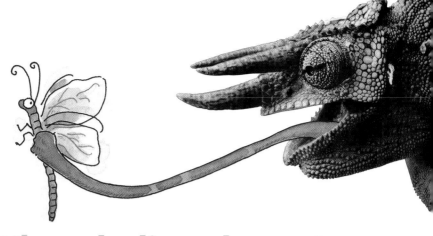

What do lizards eat?

Most lizards eat insects.

Some eat spiders, snails,

worms, slugs, or mice.

A few eat only plants.

Most lizards have short tongues.

But a chameleon's tongue

is longer than its body!

Its sticky tongue darts out

to catch a bug so fast

that you won't see it happen.

Blue-Tongued Skink

How well can lizards see, hear, and smell?

Most lizards have good eyesight
and good hearing.
Some lizards have ears you can see.
Others have ears under the skin
behind their eyes.
Like snakes, lizards use their tongues
to smell their surroundings.

Tokay Gecko

Do lizards ever lose their tails?

There are weak places in a lizard's tail

where it can break off.

A lizard can grow a new tail,

but the new tail will be weaker.

Some lizards can drop their tails

on purpose to protect themselves.

A surprised animal will watch

the loose, wiggling tail as the lizard escapes.

Gecko

How do lizards protect themselves?

Lizards run or climb away

from danger if they can.

Some lizards pretend to be dead

so enemies will leave them alone.

A chuckwalla hides in a small space,

then puffs itself up

until it's too big to be pulled out.

Chuckwalla

Frilled Lizard

Lizards may try to look big and scary.
A frilled lizard widens the skin
around its neck to make it look larger.
Other lizards bite or
whip enemies with their tails.
The Mexican beaded lizard and
the Gila (HEE-lah) monster
can kill with their poisonous bites.

Gecko

What unusual things can lizards do?

Geckos lick their own eyeballs clean.

Very tiny hooks on a gecko's toes

help it climb up window glass

or even crawl across a ceiling!

A flying dragon lizard spreads out

flaps of skin on its sides like wings

to glide a short way through the air.

A chameleon's skin color and pattern
can change.
This helps it to blend in
with its surroundings.
Each eye on a chameleon can look
in a different direction.
The basilisk lizard spreads its toes
to run across the top of a pond.

Turtles

Box Turtle

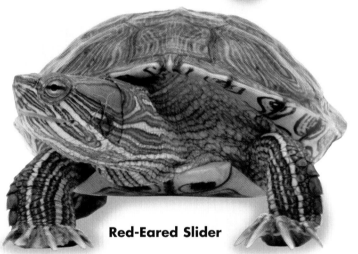

Red-Eared Slider

Wood Turtle

How many kinds of turtles are there?

There are about 250
kinds of turtles.
Some well-known turtles are
box turtles, red-eared sliders,
and snapping turtles.

Common Snapping Turtle

Bog Turtle

What are the smallest and biggest turtles?

The bog turtle is only

about three inches long

and weighs one-fourth of a pound.

The leatherback turtle

can grow to eight feet long

and weigh as much as 2,000 pounds!

Leatherback Turtle

Why do turtles have shells?

Turtles tuck their heads

and legs inside their hard shells

to protect them from enemies

and bad weather.

A turtle can never leave its shell.

Most of the shell is alive

and will grow bigger

as the turtle gets older.

Are turtles and tortoises different?

Most turtles spend time in the water
and have webbed toes for swimming.
Tortoises live on land.
Their toes aren't webbed.
A turtle's shell is usually flatter
than a tortoise's shell.

Tortoise

Turtle

Sea Turtle

How long can a turtle stay out of the water?

All turtles need to breathe air.

But they may become sick

if they are out of the water too long.

Sea turtles can stay underwater

for an hour or more.

Then they have to come up for air.

Some turtles can stay on land

for only fifteen minutes at a time.

How well can turtles see, hear, and smell?

Turtles have good eyesight

and can tell some colors apart.

They hear low, deep sounds best.

Their ears are hidden under

the skin near their eyes.

Turtles have a good sense of smell,

even under water.

This helps them find food

and stay far away from enemies.

How do turtles eat?

Most turtles eat in the water.

Water pushes food

into a turtle's mouth.

A turtle does not have teeth,

so it crushes the food

with its strong jaws.

Then water helps push the food

down into its stomach.

Turtles may eat worms, insects, plants,

fish, snails, slugs, fruits, or vegetables.

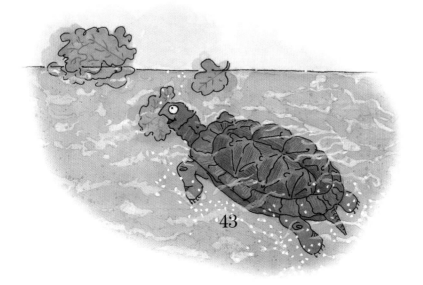

Collared Lizard

What should I know before getting a pet reptile?

All reptiles need food, water, light, proper shelter, and veterinary care. Find out everything you can about a reptile before you buy it.

How long will it live?

Box turtles can live eighty years!

How big will it get?

Young green iguanas

are only six inches long,

but they grow to five feet long.

What does it eat?

Some reptiles must be fed

live insects or mice!

Always wash your hands before

and after touching a reptile.

Some carry bacteria

or disease.

Are reptiles in danger?

Many reptiles are already extinct.

Some reptiles are in danger because

forests, ponds, and other habitats are

being destroyed, polluted, or changed.

Once a type of reptile is gone,

it is gone from the Earth forever.

Endangered Short-Horned Lizard

Endangered Hawks-Bill Sea Turtle

Which reptiles make the best pets?

Reptiles that are gentle and easy to feed and that don't get too big are best for beginners.

Ask your vet or an expert at a pet store which kind of snake, lizard, or turtle might be the right pet for you.